This Journal is the Property of

Table of Contents

Title	Page#

Table of Contents

Title	Page#

Made in United States
Troutdale, OR
12/05/2023

15370199R00058